WEEKLY PLANNER

MON ◯

TUE  ◯

WED  ◯

THU  ◯

FRI  ◯

SAT ◯

SUN ◯

Notes:

WEEKLY PLANNER

MON

TUE

WED

THU

FRI

SAT

SUN

Notes :

WEEKLY PLANNER

MON

TUE

WED

THU

FRI

SAT

SUN

Notes :

WEEKLY PLANNER

MON ◯

TUE ◯

WED ◯

THU ◯

FRI ◯

SAT ◯

SUN ◯

Notes :

WEEKLY PLANNER

MON ◯

TUE ◯

WED ◯

THU ◯

FRI ◯

SAT ◯

SUN ◯

Notes :

WEEKLY PLANNER

MON ◯

TUE ◯

WED ◯

THU ◯

FRI ◯

SAT ◯

SUN ◯

Notes:

WEEKLY PLANNER

MON

TUE

WED

THU

FRI

SAT

SUN

Notes:

WEEKLY PLANNER

MON

TUE

WED

THU

FRI

SAT

SUN

Notes:

WEEKLY PLANNER

MON

TUE

WED

THU

FRI

SAT

SUN

Notes:

WEEKLY PLANNER

MON ◯

TUE ◯

WED ◯

THU ◯

FRI ◯

SAT ◯

SUN ◯

Notes :

WEEKLY PLANNER

MON

TUE

WED

THU

FRI

SAT

SUN

Notes :

WEEKLY PLANNER

MON ◯

TUE ◯

WED ◯

THU ◯

FRI ◯

SAT ◯

SUN ◯

Notes :

WEEKLY PLANNER

MON

TUE

WED

THU

FRI

SAT

SUN

Notes:

WEEKLY PLANNER

MON

TUE

WED

THU

FRI

SAT

SUN

Notes:

WEEKLY PLANNER

MON

TUE

WED

THU

FRI

SAT

SUN

Notes :

WEEKLY PLANNER

MON ◯

TUE ◯

WED ◯

THU ◯

FRI ◯

SAT ◯

SUN ◯

Notes :

WEEKLY PLANNER

MON

TUE

WED

THU

FRI

SAT

SUN

Notes :

WEEKLY PLANNER

MON

TUE

WED

THU

FRI

SAT

SUN

Notes :

WEEKLY PLANNER

MON

TUE

WED

THU

FRI

SAT

SUN

Notes :

WEEKLY PLANNER

MON

TUE

WED

THU

FRI

SAT

SUN

Notes:

WEEKLY PLANNER

MON

TUE

WED

THU

FRI

SAT

SUN

Notes:

WEEKLY PLANNER

MON

TUE

WED

THU

FRI

SAT

SUN

Notes:

WEEKLY PLANNER

MON

TUE

WED

THU

FRI

SAT

SUN

Notes :

WEEKLY PLANNER

MON

TUE

WED

THU

FRI

SAT

SUN

Notes :

WEEKLY PLANNER

MON ○

TUE ○

WED ○

THU ○

FRI ○

SAT ○

SUN ○

Notes :

WEEKLY PLANNER

MON

TUE

WED

THU

FRI

SAT

SUN

Notes :

WEEKLY PLANNER

MON

TUE

WED

THU

FRI

SAT

SUN

Notes :

WEEKLY PLANNER

MON ◯

TUE ◯

WED ◯

THU ◯

FRI ◯

SAT ◯

SUN ◯

Notes:

WEEKLY PLANNER

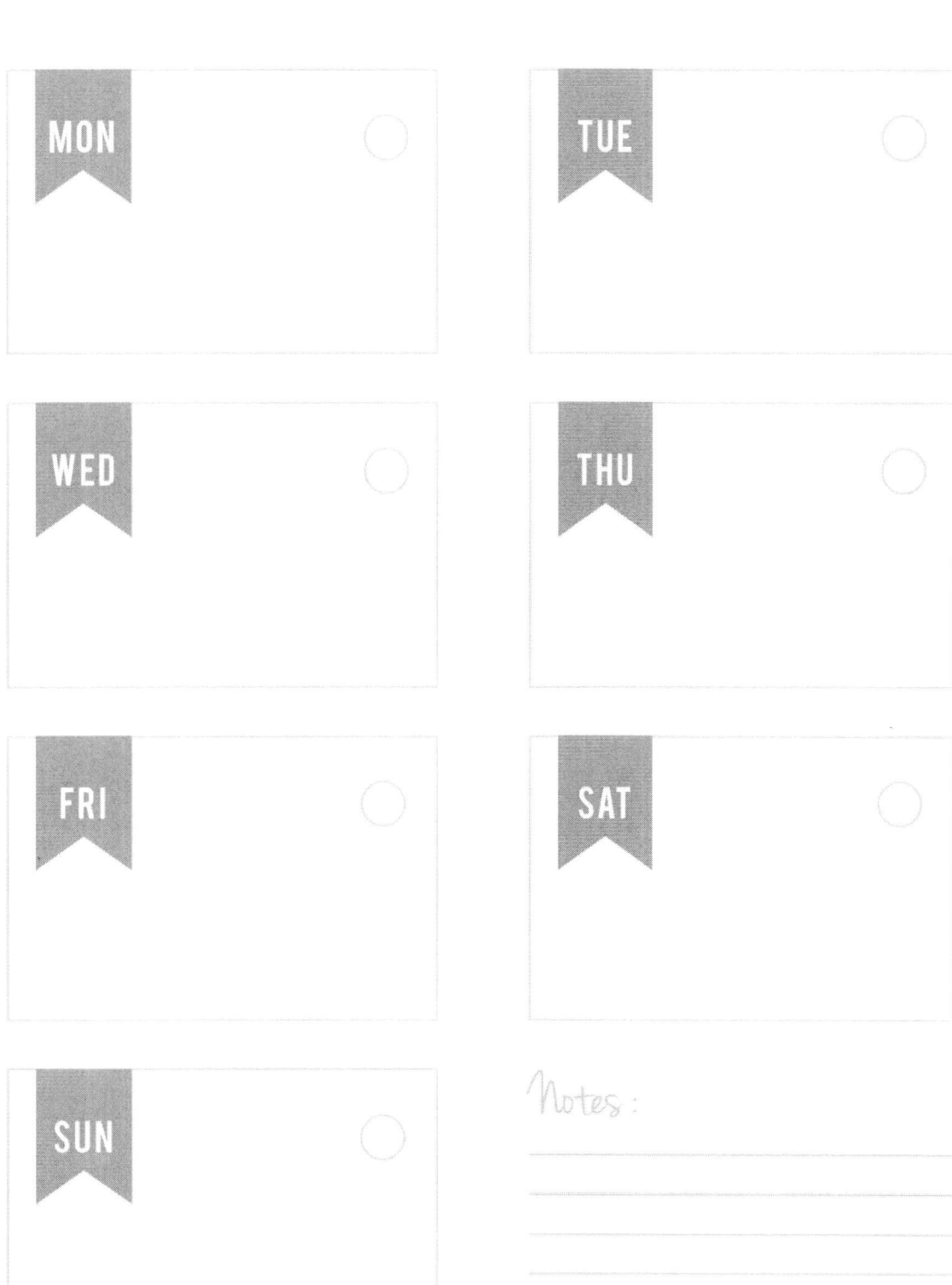

MON

TUE

WED

THU

FRI

SAT

SUN

Notes:

WEEKLY PLANNER

MON ◯

TUE ◯

WED ◯

THU ◯

FRI ◯

SAT ◯

SUN ◯

Notes:

WEEKLY PLANNER

MON

TUE

WED

THU

FRI

SAT

SUN

Notes :

WEEKLY PLANNER

MON

TUE

WED

THU

FRI

SAT

SUN

Notes :

WEEKLY PLANNER

MON

TUE

WED

THU

FRI

SAT

SUN

Notes :

WEEKLY PLANNER

MON

TUE

WED

THU

FRI

SAT

SUN

Notes :

WEEKLY PLANNER

MON

TUE

WED

THU

FRI

SAT

SUN

Notes :

The following 10 Images are taken from Creative Engagements Coloring Books titled

- It's Tea Time
- English Garden Party
- Antique Hunting

MAKE DO
& MEND

WEEKLY PLANNER

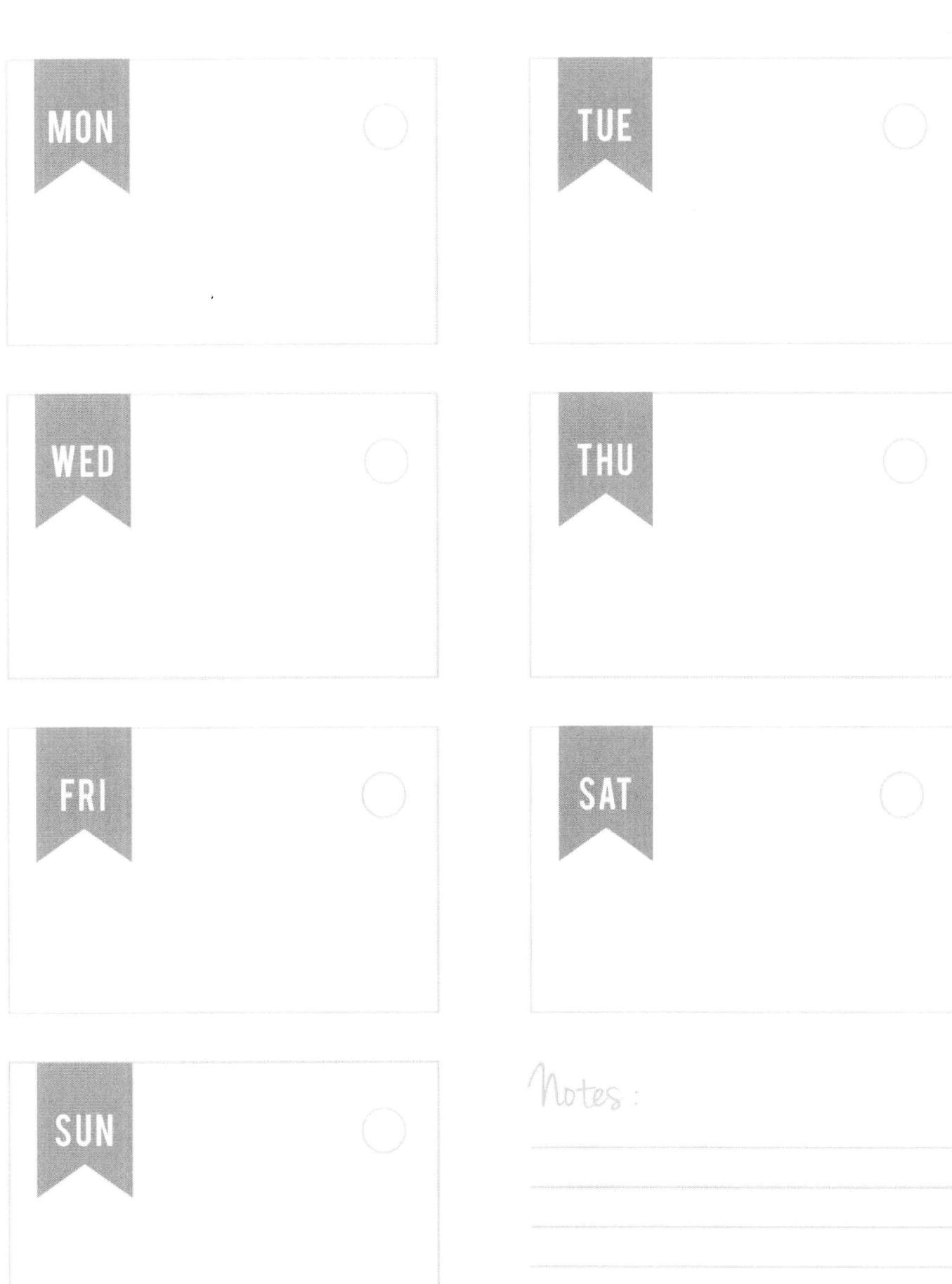

MON

TUE

WED

THU

FRI

SAT

SUN

Notes:

WEEKLY PLANNER

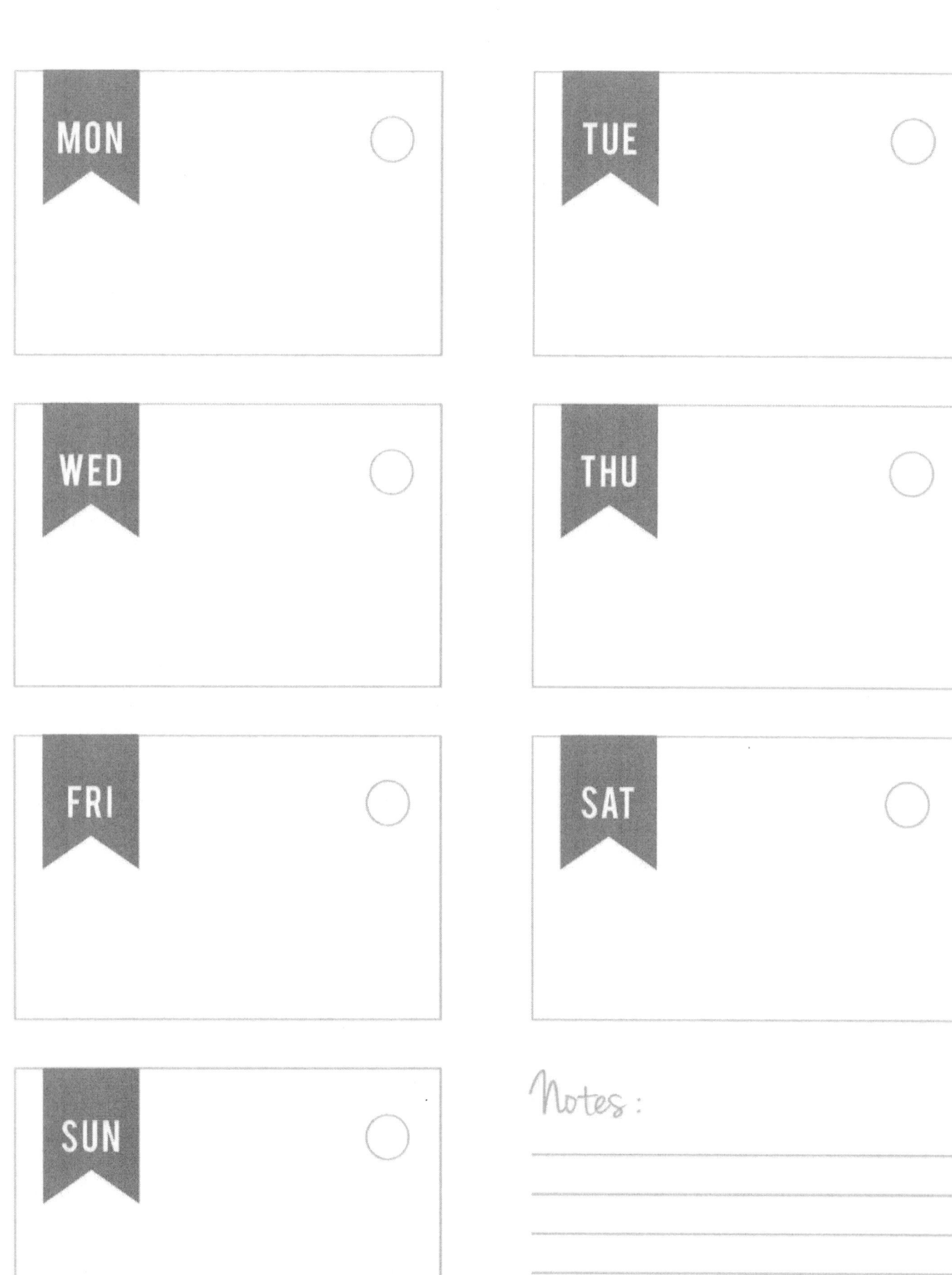

MON

TUE

WED

THU

FRI

SAT

SUN

Notes:

WEEKLY PLANNER

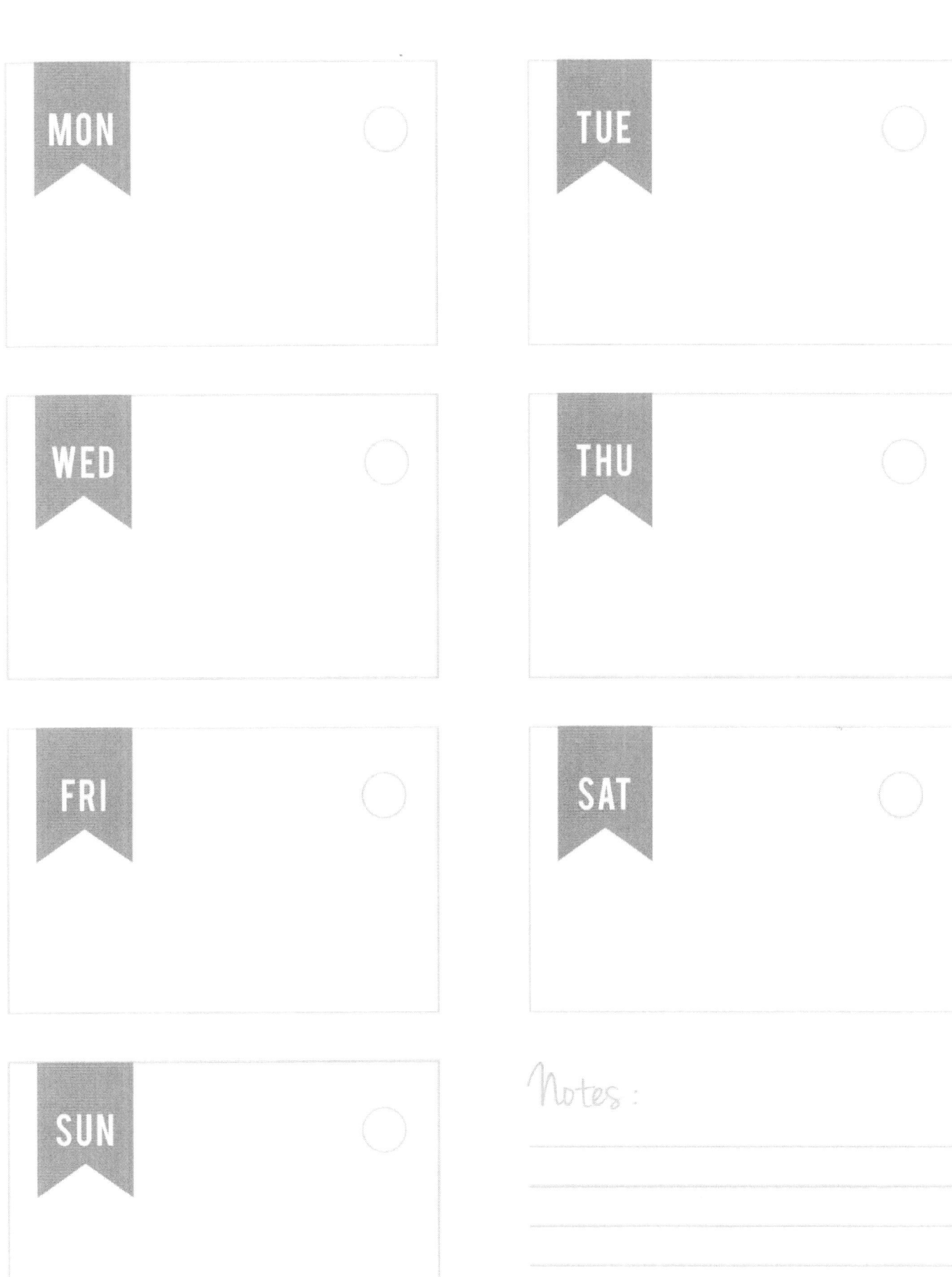

MON

TUE

WED

THU

FRI

SAT

SUN

Notes :

WEEKLY PLANNER

MON

TUE

WED

THU

FRI

SAT

SUN

Notes:

WEEKLY PLANNER

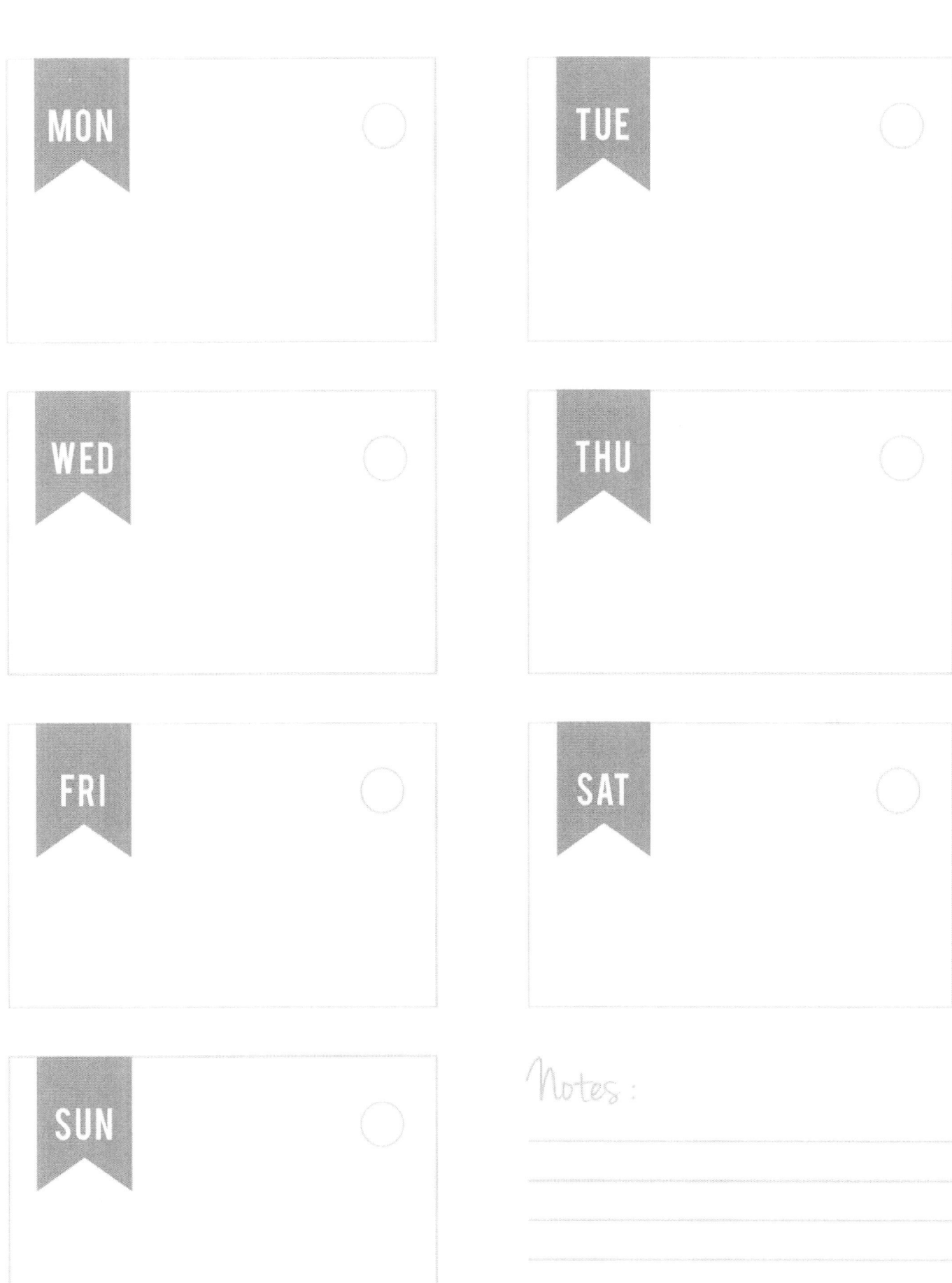

MON

TUE

WED

THU

FRI

SAT

SUN

Notes :

WEEKLY PLANNER

MON

TUE

WED

THU

FRI

SAT

SUN

Notes :

WEEKLY PLANNER

MON

TUE

WED

THU

FRI

SAT

SUN

Notes:

WEEKLY PLANNER

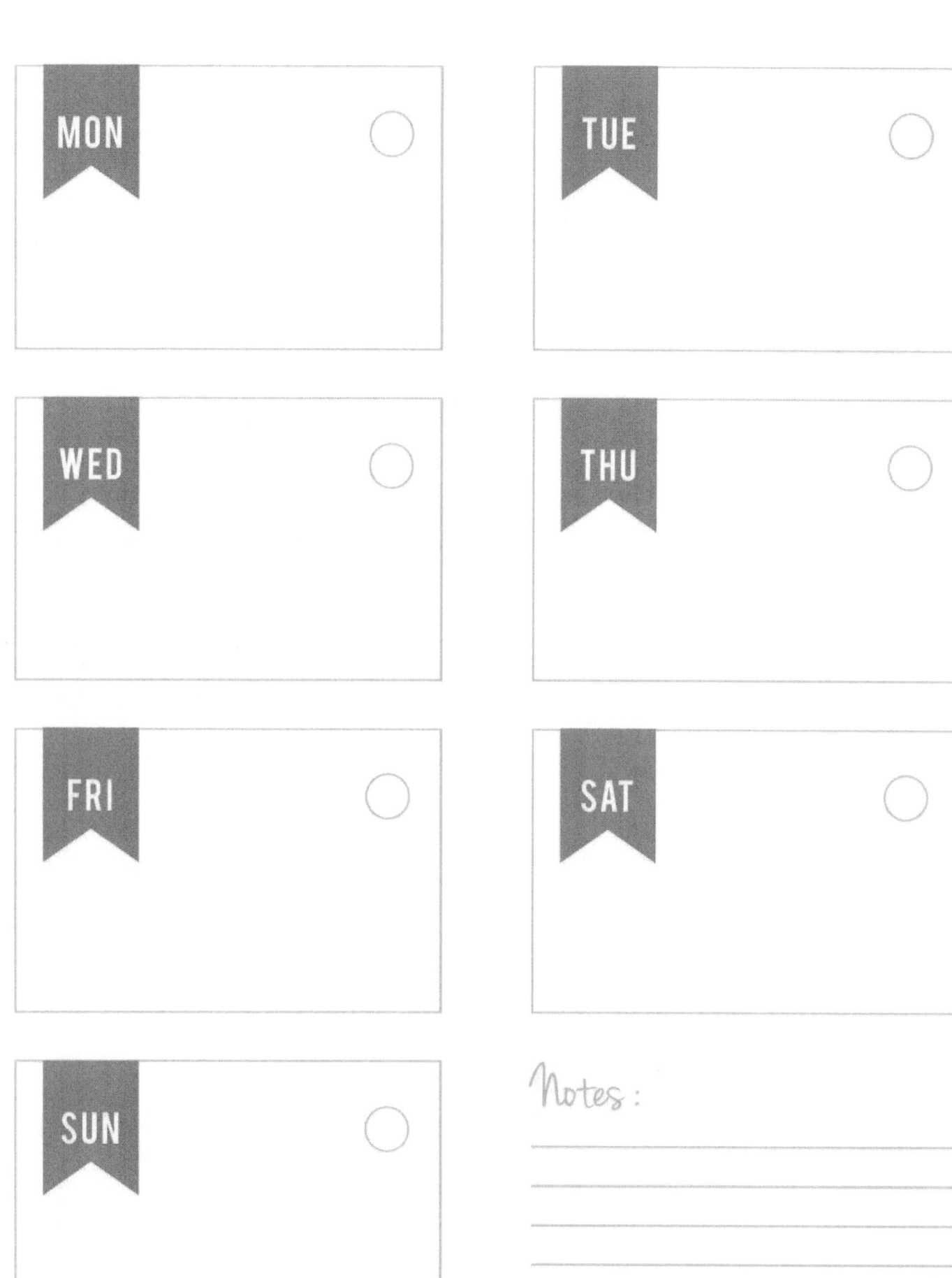

MON

TUE

WED

THU

FRI

SAT

SUN

Notes :

WEEKLY PLANNER

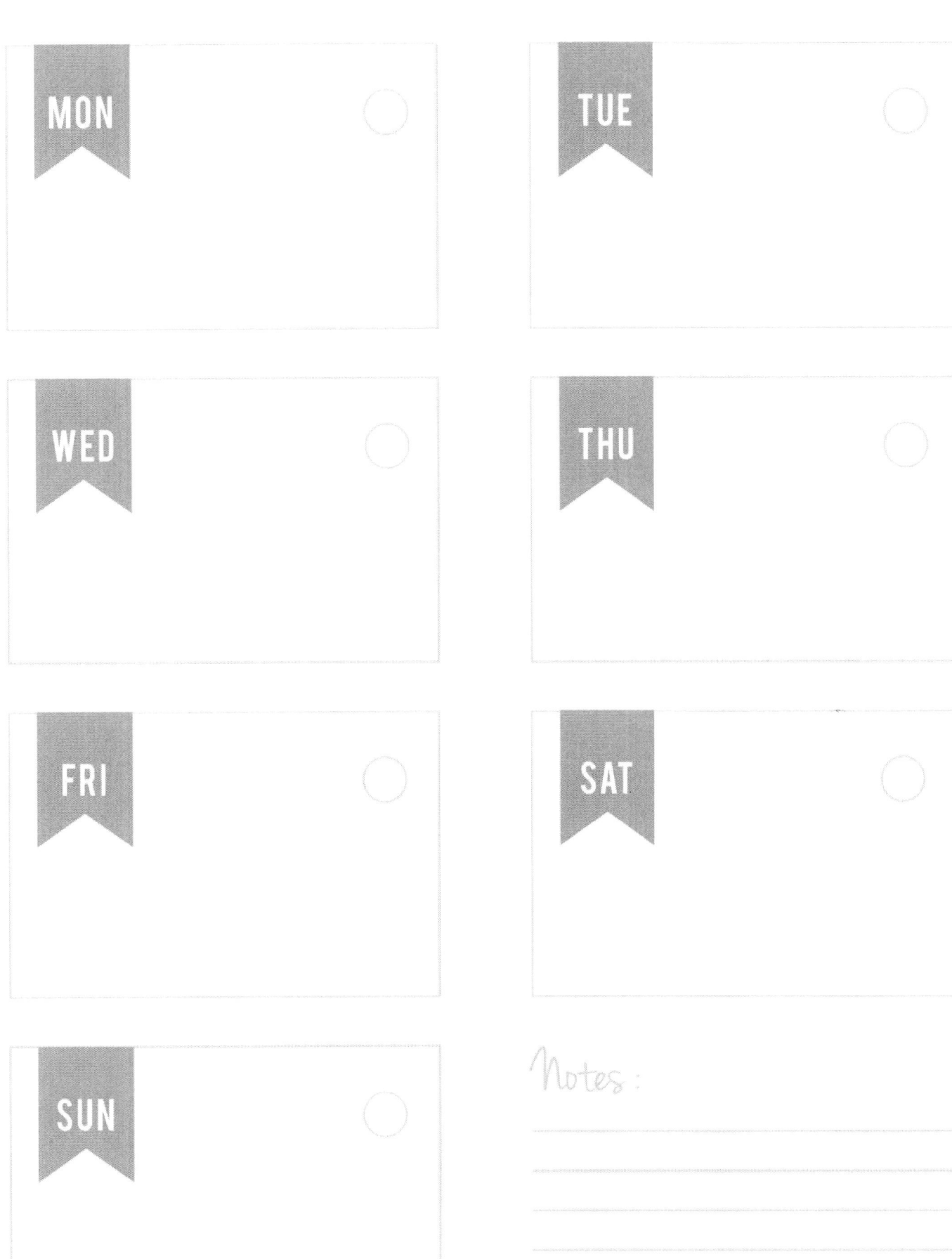

MON

TUE

WED

THU

FRI

SAT

SUN

Notes:

WEEKLY PLANNER

MON

TUE

WED

THU

FRI

SAT

SUN

Notes:

WEEKLY PLANNER

MON

TUE

WED

THU

FRI

SAT

SUN

Notes:

WEEKLY PLANNER

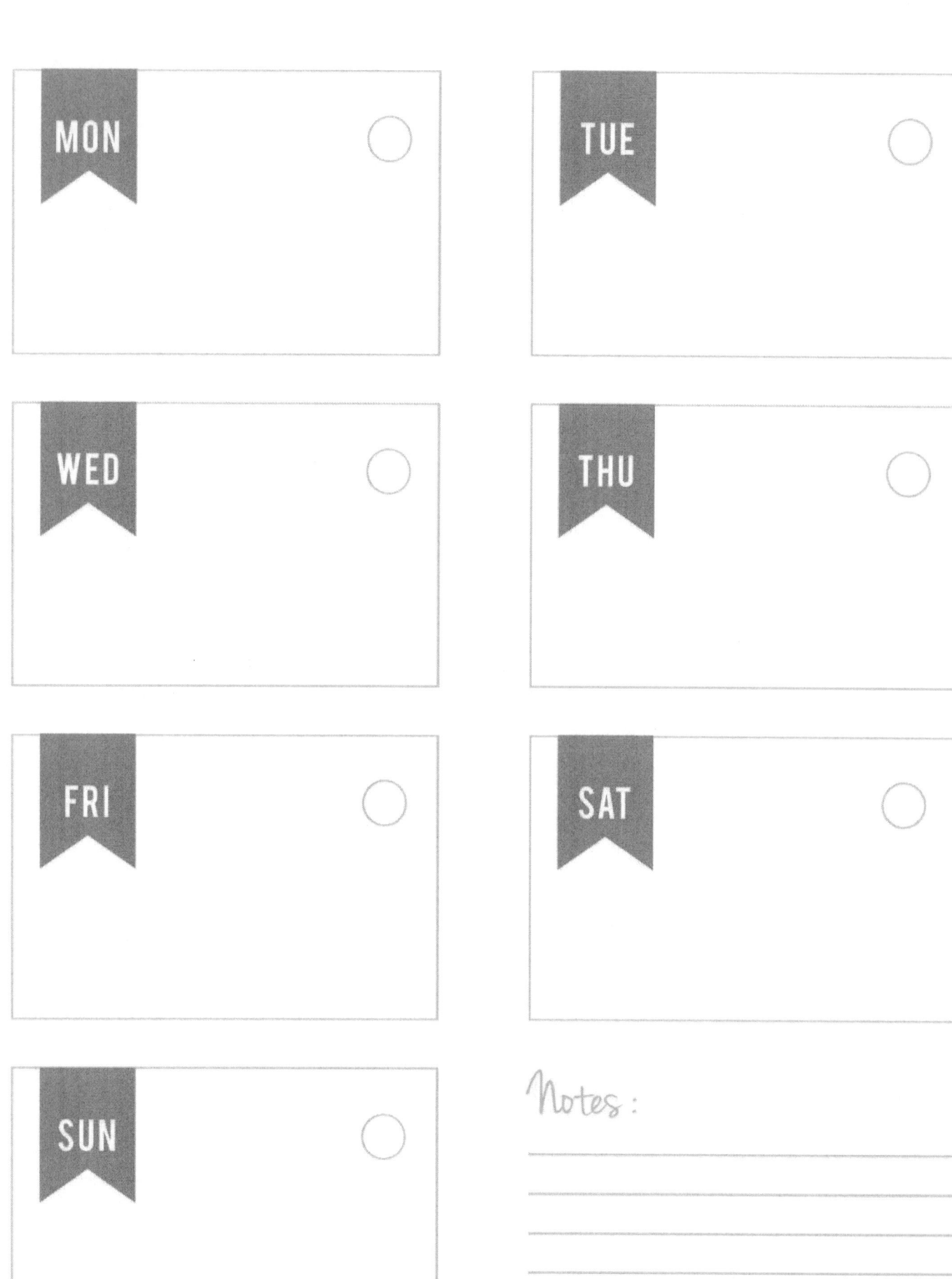

MON

TUE

WED

THU

FRI

SAT

SUN

Notes:

WEEKLY PLANNER

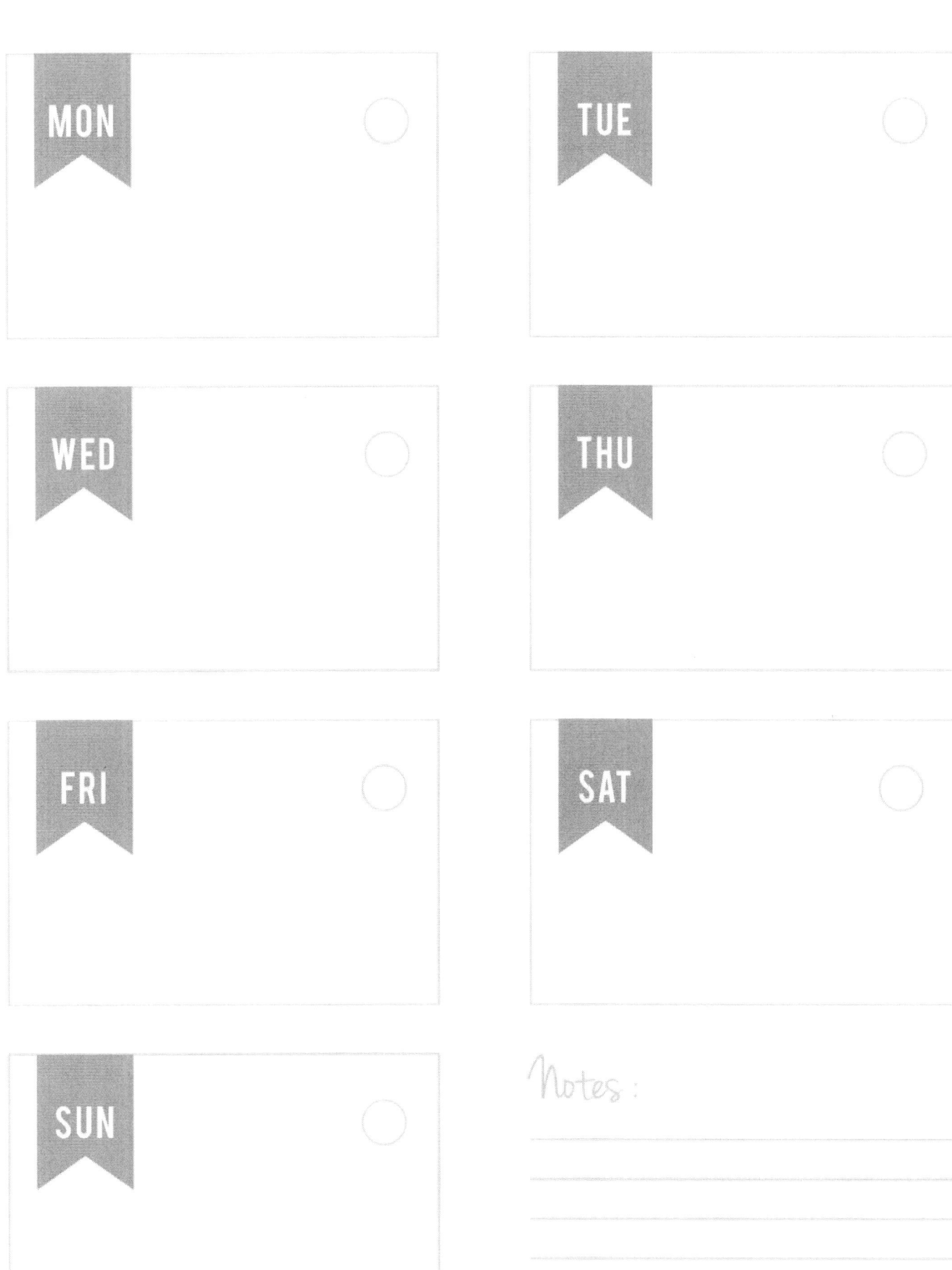

MON

TUE

WED

THU

FRI

SAT

SUN

Notes:

WEEKLY PLANNER

MON

TUE

WED

THU

FRI

SAT

SUN

Notes:

WEEKLY PLANNER

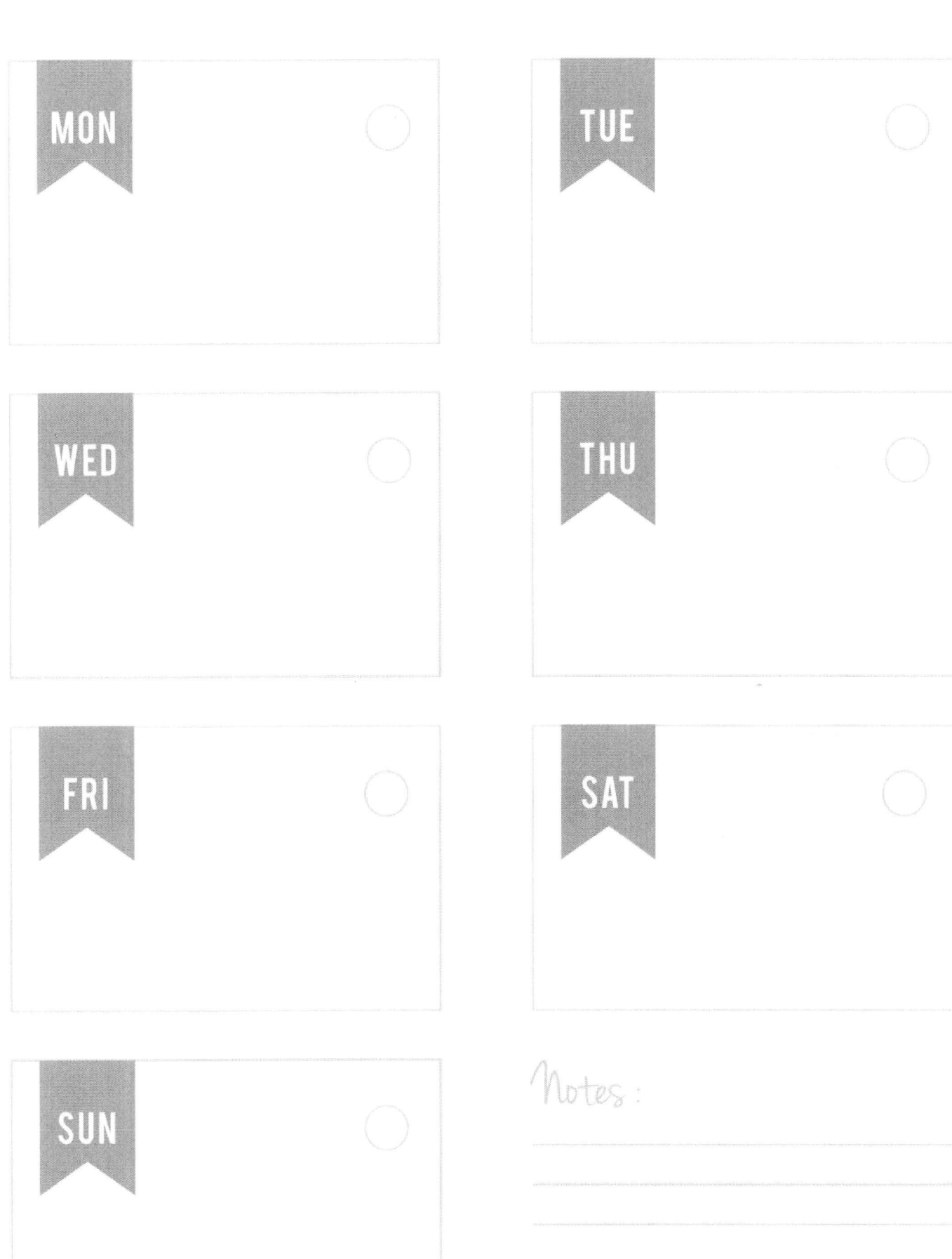

MON

TUE

WED

THU

FRI

SAT

SUN

Notes:

WEEKLY PLANNER

MON

TUE

WED

THU

FRI

SAT

SUN

Notes:

WEEKLY PLANNER

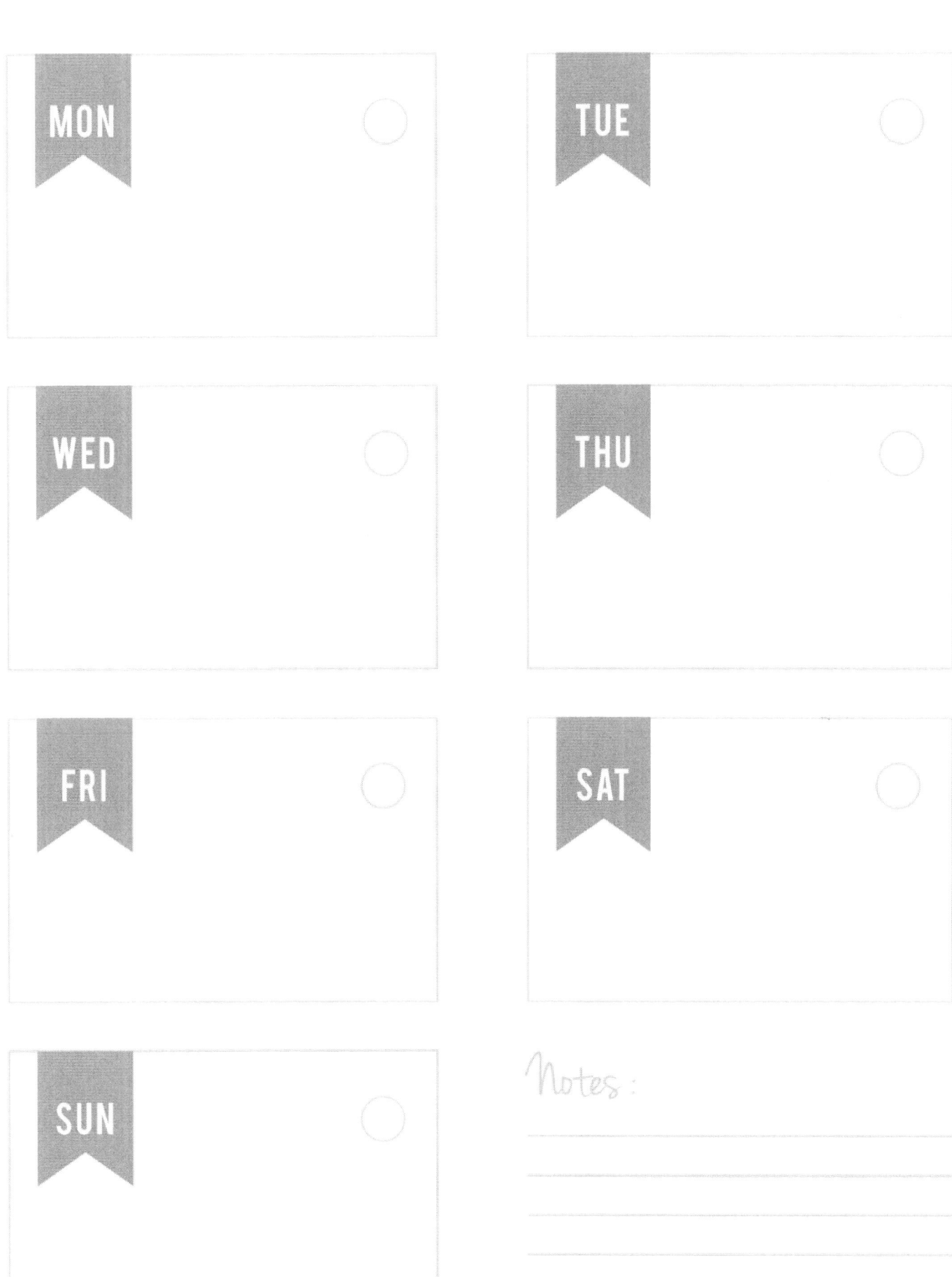

MON

TUE

WED

THU

FRI

SAT

SUN

Notes:

WEEKLY PLANNER

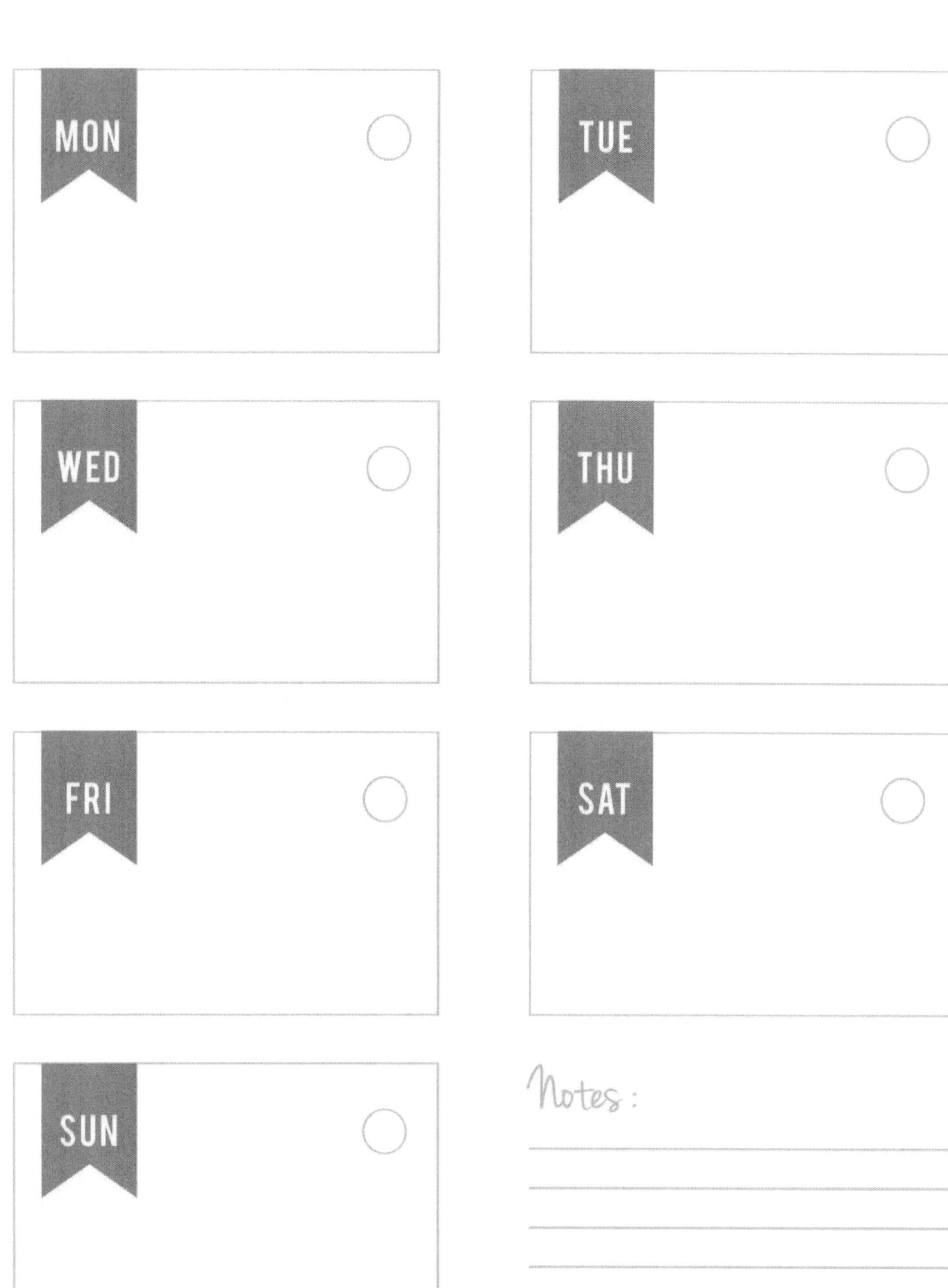

MON

TUE

WED

THU

FRI

SAT

SUN

Notes:

WEEKLY PLANNER

MON

TUE

WED

THU

FRI

SAT

SUN

Notes:

WEEKLY PLANNER

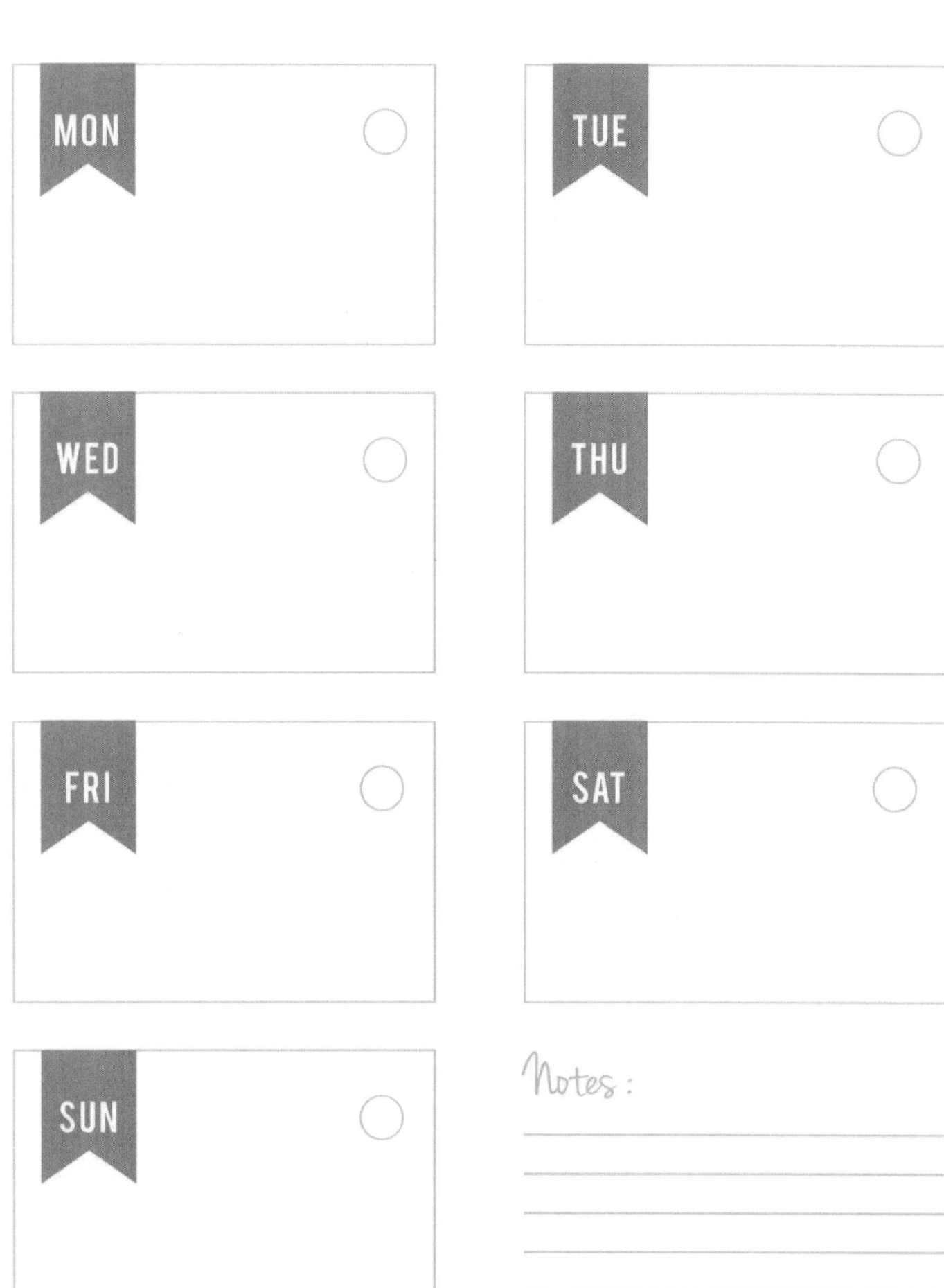

MON

TUE

WED

THU

FRI

SAT

SUN

Notes:

Sketch Pad

Thank you for purchasing a Creative Engagements Coloring Book. For wonderful results, clear a special place to color and place all your colored pencils, markers and fine tipped markers nearby. Relax and let your mind create as you let the stress of the day float away. Use different media as a way to "think outside the box" and to discover colorful art like never before. Also, you may want to place a blank sheet of paper behind the page you are coloring so the ink does not bleed through.

Extra coloring pages have been provided for you to "tear and share" with the ones you love! Celebrate the moment together! Some of our books are also available on Kindle. If you purchased this book, you may also use your Kindle to download a copy of it and print out any art you wish to color again. Simply find us on Amazon.com and select "Kindle Version" to download the book. Some books are not Kindle supported.

Relax, re-create your life and enjoy color!

Printed in Great Britain
by Amazon